5/2014

LAFOURCHE PARISH PUBLIC LIBRARY

0 0533 0064 2784 3

W9-BZU-786

4

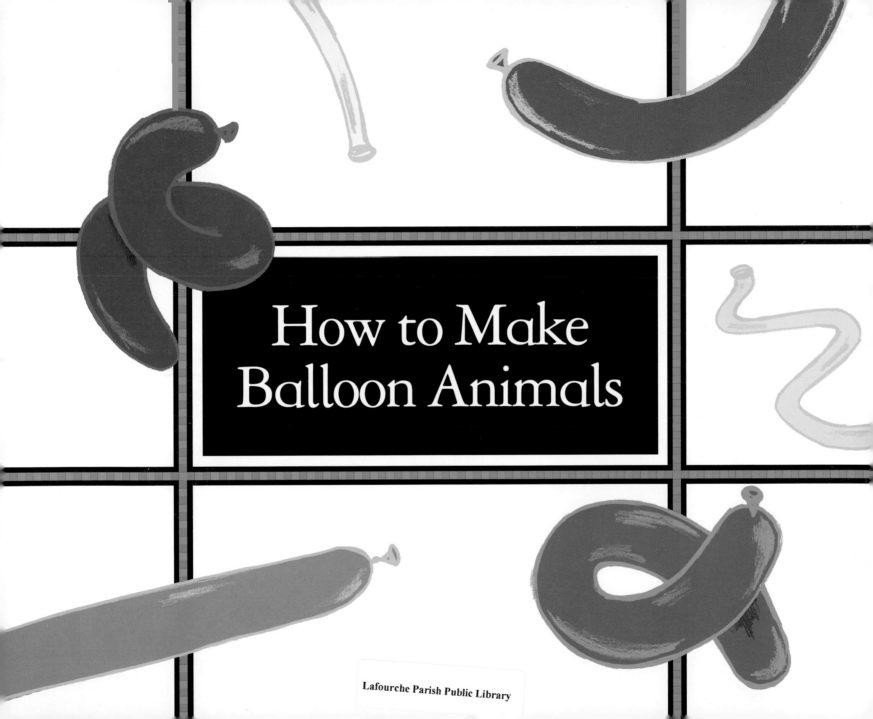

How to Make
Balloon Animals

Lafourche Parish Public Library

The Child's World

Published by The Child's World®
1980 Lookout Drive • Mankato, MN 56003-1705
800-599-READ • www.childsworld.com

Acknowledgments
The Child's World®: Mary Berendes, Publishing Director
Red Line Editorial: Editorial direction and production
The Design Lab: Design

Photographs ©: Johanna Goodyear/Shutterstock Images, 4

Copyright © 2014 by The Child's World®
All rights reserved. No part of this book may be reproduced or utilized in
any form or by any means without written permission from the publisher.

ISBN: 978-1623235581
LCCN: 2013931423

Printed in the United States of America
Mankato, MN
July, 2013
PA02176

ABOUT THE AUTHOR
Megan Atwood lives in Saint Paul, Minnesota, with two cats. She makes balloon shapes whenever she can.

ABOUT THE ILLUSTRATOR
Kelsey Oseid is an illustrator and graphic designer from Minneapolis, Minnesota. When she's not drawing, she likes to do craft projects, bake cookies, go on walks, and play with her two cats, Jamie and Fiona. You can find her work at www.kelseyoseid.com.

Table of Contents

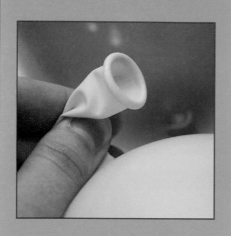

TYING YOUR BALLOON

First, stretch out your balloon a few times until it's nice and flexible. Then blow it up using your balloon pump. Hold on to the tie end. Then wrap it around your first finger and your middle finger. Put the end of the balloon through the space between your first and second fingers. The more you practice, the better you will be at tying your balloon!

It's Balloon Time!

Have you ever watched a clown make shapes out of balloons? Did you know that you can do it, too? This book will teach you how. We'll start with a few basic projects. Then we'll move on to some awesome animals. Get ready to impress your friends with your balloon-twisting skills!

You'll need a few tools before you start. You can ask your parents to help you find them in a store or online.

For the projects in this book, you'll need:

- Long, skinny balloons for making shapes
- 1 round party balloon
- A balloon pump

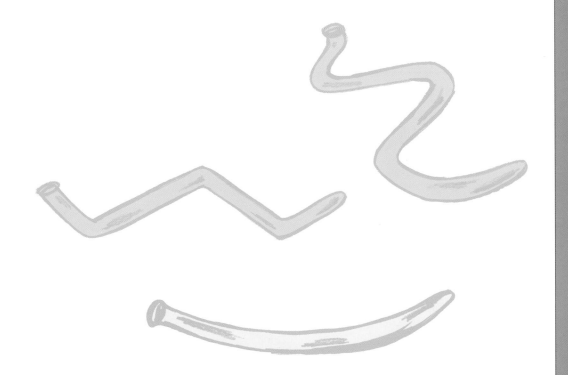

SAFETY TIPS
It's always important to stay safe. Balloons can pop. Popping can be dangerous if it happens near your eyes. Make sure you hold the balloon away from you. Ask an adult to help you the first few times you make your balloon shapes.

Balloon Sword

Your first project will teach you some easy balloon-twisting tricks. Swords can be dangerous. Let's make one that's as light as air.

Use whatever color balloon you want. Remember to stretch your balloon out before blowing it up. Leave a bit of room at the tip of the balloon. That way the balloon's air has a place to go if the twisting gets too tight. Tie the end of your balloon. Now you're ready to go!

1
Put your hand up to the tie end of your **inflated** balloon. Look at where your pinkie finger hits. This is where you will put your first twist.

STEP 1

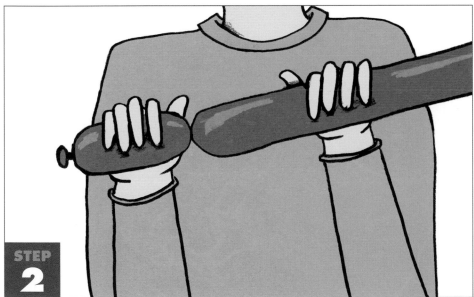

STEP 2

2
Twist the balloon. Now you should have two **segments**, one long and one short.

3 Now fold up the long segment of the balloon. The crease should be about a pinkie's length away from the **step 2** twist.

4 Make another twist near the **step 2** twist to create part of a handle.

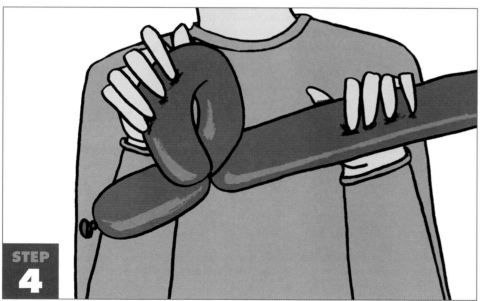

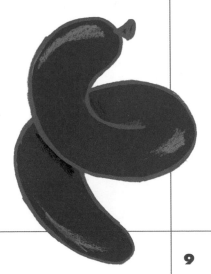

5 Now just do the same thing on the other side! Twist the balloon into the twist where the first loop is.

Now you're ready for a super-safe sword fight!

WHAT YOU'LL NEED:
• 1 long balloon
• Balloon pump

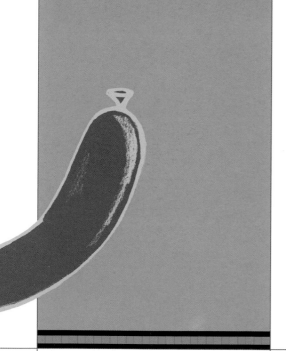

Unicorn Horn

Now it's time to twist a balloon into something you can wear. Follow the steps below to make a magical **unicorn** horn.

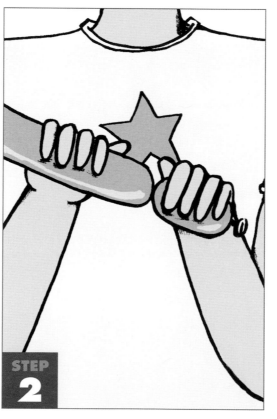

STEP
2

1 Pick a balloon of whatever color you want. Then blow it up. Remember to leave a bit of space at the tip!

2 Hold your pinkie finger up against the tie end of the balloon. Make a twist where your pinkie ends.

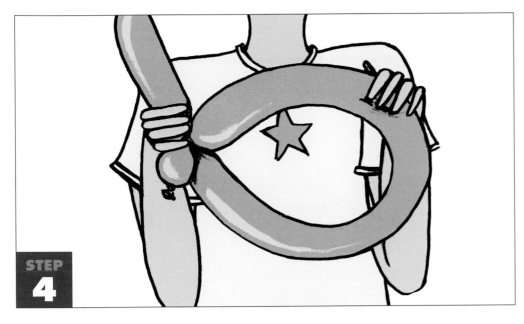

3 Now take your **step** 2 twist and make a loop with the rest of the balloon. The loop should fit around your head.

4 Now take your **step** 2 twist and twist it into the rest of the balloon.

5 Place the loop on your head so the horn is in front.

Easy! You just made a sharp-looking unicorn horn.

STEP **4**

STEP **5**

WHAT YOU'LL NEED:
- 1 long balloon
- 1 round party balloon
- Balloon pump

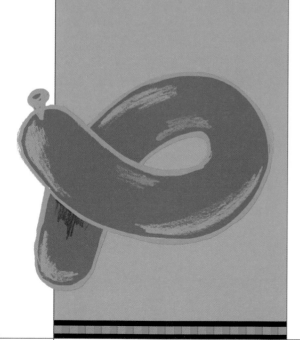

Balloon Fish

Have you ever wished for an inflatable fish? It's your lucky day!

This project will use two balloons. You'll need one long balloon and one round party balloon.

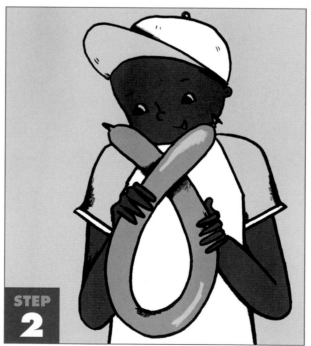

STEP 2

1 We'll start by making the fish's body. Blow up your long balloon. Make sure to leave a little bit of space in the tip.

2 Fold the balloon in half.

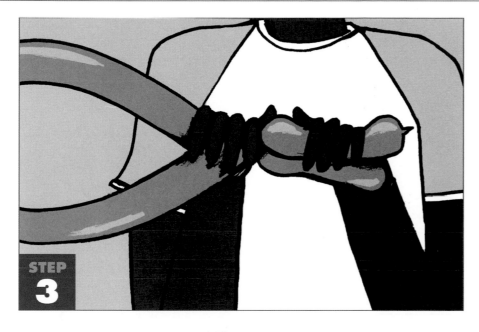

3 Twist the two ends together about a hand's length from the end of the balloon. Your fish has a body!

4 Now blow up the round party balloon. Make it big enough that it will fit snugly inside the loop you made in **step 3**. The party balloon will be your fish's belly!

5 Carefully put the inflated round balloon inside your fish's body.

Now try putting your fish in the bathtub or a pool. He floats!

Balloon Dog

WHAT YOU'LL NEED:
- 1 long balloon
- Balloon pump

Have you ever wanted a balloon pet? Here's your chance! Follow the steps below to make your own dog out of a balloon.

1 Pick whatever color balloon you want. Blow it up. Leave about two to three fingers of space at the tip.

2 Measure about two hands up from the tie end of the balloon. Fold the balloon there.

STEP 2

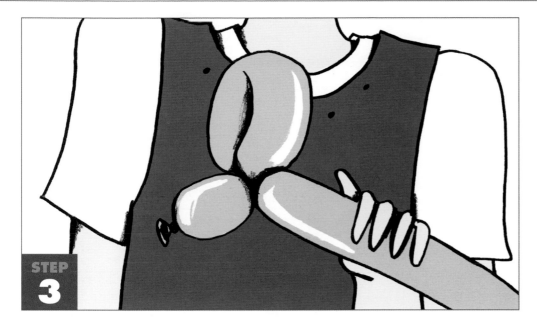

STEP
3

3 Now make a twist about four fingers from the folded end of the balloon. You just made the dog's ears and **snout**!

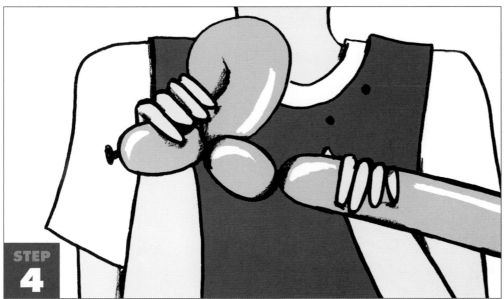

STEP
4

4 Measure three fingers from the last twist. Make another twist at this spot. This will be the dog's neck.

Lafourche Parish Public Library

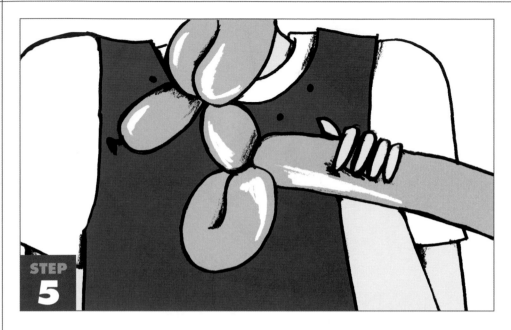

5 Now fold up the balloon again like you did in **step** 1. Twist the folded section into the last twist you made. This will make the dog's front legs.

6 Now it's time for the back end! Measure about a hand's length away from your last twist. Make another twist here.

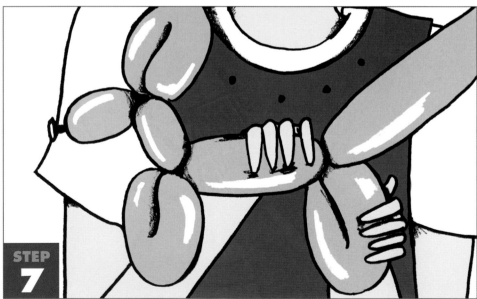

7 Now fold the rest of the balloon in a loop.

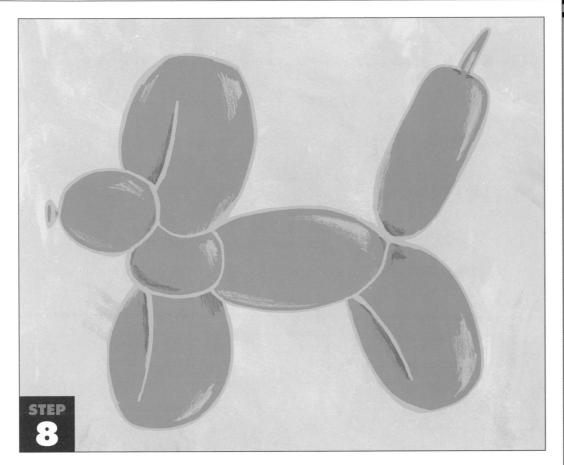

STEP
8

8 Twist the loop into your last twist. Now your dog has back legs and a tail.

Say hello to your new dog! Now all you need to do is give her a name.

MAKE A GIRAFFE
Real giraffes and dogs don't really look alike. But a balloon giraffe is just a yellow dog with an extra-long neck! You can make a giraffe by making the neck longer than you would for a balloon dog. Instead of measuring three fingers from the head in **step 4**, measure two hands' lengths. Easy!

Monkey and Banana

WHAT YOU'LL NEED:
- 2 long balloons (1 brown balloon and 1 yellow balloon look the most like a monkey and a banana, so that's what the instructions say to use. But you can use any colors you want!)
- Balloon pump

Are you ready for a monkey? This is a hard one. You might want to ask an adult to help you.

STEP 3

1 Start by blowing up a brown balloon. Leave space at the tip of the balloon. This space should be about one-and-a-half hands long.

2 Next blow up a yellow balloon. Leave about two fingers of space at the tip of the balloon.

3 Now let's make the monkey's head. Start by

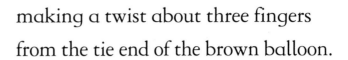

making a twist about three fingers from the tie end of the brown balloon.

4 Measure four fingers from the twist you made in **step** 3. Fold the balloon here. Then twist your **step 3** twist into the fold. You've made the monkey's head and ears.

5 Now for the body! Make a twist about three fingers down from the head. This will be the monkey's neck.

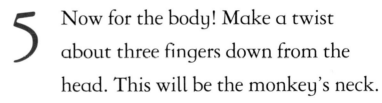

6 Fold the rest of the balloon to make a loop. Make sure the loop is big enough to hold a banana! Twist this loop into the twist you made in **step 5**.

STEP 7

7 Now make the back legs. Make another twist about a hand's length down the balloon. This will be the monkey's body. Twist the rest of your balloon to make another loop here. This loop should be about the same size as your front loop. Twist to form the monkey's legs.

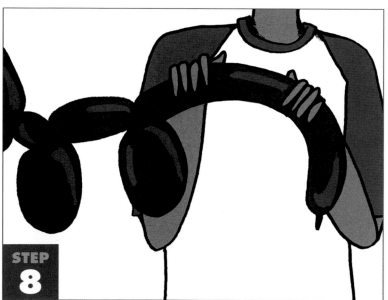

STEP 8

8 Now all that's left is the tail! Carefully squeeze the rest of the balloon. Gently curve it so the air goes into the tip. You have a monkey!

STEP 9

9 Now for the best part! Monkeys love bananas. Just slide the yellow balloon through the monkey's legs.

Now you have a happy monkey!

CLEANING UP
What's the best thing about balloon animals? There's hardly anything to clean up! Make sure to put your balloon creations in a safe place where they won't pop. Put away any extra balloons and the air pump. And guess what? You're done!

Glossary

inflated (in-FLATE-ed): An object is inflated when it has been expanded by putting air into it. You can turn an inflated balloon into many different shapes.

segments (SEG-muhntz): Segments are sections of something. Twisting a balloon into segments can make a fun shape.

snout (SNOUT): A snout is the front part of an animal's head. A snout includes the nose, mouth, and jaws.

unicorn (YOO-ni-korn): A unicorn is an imaginary animal that looks like a horse with a horn. You can make your own unicorn hat using a balloon.

Learn More

Books

Chauffe, Emily and Elizabeth. *Kids Show Kids How to Make Balloon Animals*. Austin, TX: Casey Shay Press, 2009.

Telford, Jeremy. *Balloonology: 32 Fun Projects to Take You From Beginner to Expert*. Layton, UT: Gibbs Smith, 2010.

Web Sites

Visit our Web site for links about balloon animals: *childsworld.com/links*

Note to Parents, Teachers, and Librarians: We routinely verify our Web links to make sure they are safe and active sites. So encourage your readers to check them out!

Index